SILENCE, JOY

Also by Thomas Merton
from New Directions

On Christian Contemplation
On Eastern Meditation
The Way of Chuang Tzu
Gandhi on Non-Violence
New Seeds of Contemplation
In the Dark Before Dawn
Bread in the Wilderness
Thoughts on the East
Thomas Merton in Alaska
The Literary Essays of Thomas Merton
The Collected Poems of Thomas Merton
My Argument with the Gestapo
The Asian Journal of Thomas Merton
The Geography of Lograire
Zen and the Birds of Appetite
Raids on the Unspeakable
The Wisdom of the Desert

SILENCE, JOY

A Selection of Writings by Thomas Merton

Edited by Christopher Wait

A New Directions Book

New Directions is grateful to Houghton Mifflin Harcourt for granting permission to reprint excerpts from *No Man Is an Island* and *The Sign of Jonas*. A full list of sources and acknowledgments can be found at the back of this volume.

Manufactured in the United States of America
New Directions Books are printed on acid-free paper
First published as a New Directions Paperbook Original in 2018
Design by Marian Bantjes

Library of Congress Cataloging-in-Publication Data
Names: Merton, Thomas, 1915–1968, author.
Title: Silence, joy : a selection of writings / by Thomas Merton.
Description: New York : New Directions Books, 2018. |
Includes bibliographical references.
Identifiers: LCCN 2018021497 (print) | LCCN 2018024120 (ebook) |
ISBN 9780811228244 (ebook) | ISBN 9780811228237 (alk. paper)
Classification: LCC PS3525.E7174 (ebook) | LCC PS3525.E7174 A6 2018 (print) | DDC 811/.54—dc23
LC record available at https://lccn.loc.gov/2018021497

10 9 8 7 6 5 4 3 2 1

New Directions Books are published for James Laughlin
by New Directions Publishing Corporation
80 Eighth Avenue, New York 10011

CONTENTS

SEEDS OF CONTEMPLATION

Every moment and every event of every man's life on earth plants something in his soul. For just as the wind carries thousands of winged seeds, so each moment brings with it germs of spiritual vitality that come to rest imperceptibly in the minds and wills of men. Most of these unnumbered seeds perish and are lost, because men are not prepared to receive them: for such seeds as these cannot spring up anywhere except in the good soil of freedom, spontaneity and love.

This is no new idea. Christ in the parable of the sower long ago told us that "The seed is the word of God." We often think this applies only to the word of the Gospel as formally preached in churches on Sundays (if indeed it is preached in churches any more!). But every expression of the will of God is in some sense a "word" of God and therefore a "seed" of new life. The ever-changing reality in the midst of which we live should awaken us to the possibility of an uninterrupted dialogue with God.

By this I do not mean continuous "talk," or a frivolously conversational form of affective prayer which is sometimes cultivated in convents, but a dialogue of love and of choice. A dialogue of deep wills.

In all the situations of life the "will of God" comes to us not merely as an external dictate of impersonal law but above all as an interior invitation of personal love. Too often the conventional conception of "God's will" as a sphinx-like and arbitrary force bearing down upon us with implacable hostility, leads men to lose faith in a God they cannot find it possible to love. Such a view of the divine will drives human weakness to despair and one wonders if it is not, itself, often the expression of a despair too intolerable to be admitted to conscious consideration. These arbitrary "dictates" of a domineering and insensible Father are more often seeds of hatred than of love. If that is our concept of the will of God, we cannot possibly seek the obscure and intimate mystery of the encounter that takes place in contemplation. We will desire only to fly as far as possible from Him and hide from His Face forever. So much depends on our idea of God!

Yet no idea of Him, however pure and perfect, is adequate to express Him as He really is. Our idea of God tells us more about ourselves than about Him.

We must learn to realize that the love of God seeks us in every situation, and seeks our good. His inscrutable love seeks our awakening. True, since this awakening implies a kind of death to our exterior self, we will dread His coming in proportion as we are identified with this exterior self and attached to it. But when we understand the dialectic of life and death we will learn to take the risks implied by faith, to make the choices that deliver us from our routine self and open to us the door of a new being, a new reality.

The mind that is the prisoner of conventional ideas, and the will that is the captive of its own desire cannot accept the seeds of an unfamiliar truth and a supernatural desire. For how can I receive the seeds of freedom if I am in love with slavery and how can I cherish the desire of God if I am filled with another and an opposite desire? God cannot plant His liberty in me because I am a prisoner and I do not even desire to be free. I love my captivity and I imprison myself in the desire for the things that I hate, and I have hardened my heart against true love. I must learn therefore to let go of the familiar and the usual and consent to what is new and unknown to me. I must learn to "leave myself" in order to find myself by yielding to the love of God. If I were looking for God, every event and every moment would sow, in my will, grains of His life that would spring up one day in a tremendous harvest.

For it is God's love that warms me in the sun and God's love that sends the cold rain. It is God's love that feeds me in the bread I eat and God that feeds me also by hunger and fasting. It is the love of God that sends the winter days when I am cold and sick, and the hot summer when I labor and my clothes are full of sweat: but it is God Who breathes on me with light winds off the river and in the breezes out of the wood. His love spreads the shade of the sycamore over my head and sends the water-boy along the edge of the wheat field with a bucket from the spring, while the laborers are resting and the mules stand under the tree.

It is God's love that speaks to me in the birds and streams; but also behind the clamor of the city God speaks to me in His judgments, and all these things are seeds sent to me from His will.

If these seeds would take root in my liberty, and if His will would grow from my freedom, I would become the love that He is, and my harvest would be His glory and my own joy.

And I would grow together with thousands and millions of other freedoms into the gold of one huge field praising God, loaded with increase, loaded with wheat. If in all things I consider only the heat and the cold, the food or the hunger, the sickness or labor, the beauty or pleasure, the success and failure or the material good or evil my works have won for my own will, I will find only emptiness and not happiness. I shall not be fed, I shall not be full. For my food is the will of Him Who made me and Who made all things in order to give Himself to me through them.

My chief care should not be to find pleasure or success, health or life or money or rest or even things like virtue and wisdom—still less their opposites, pain, failure, sickness, death. But in all that happens, my one desire and my one joy should be to know: "Here is the thing that God has willed for me. In this His love is found, and in accepting this I can give back His love to Him and give myself with it to Him. For in giving myself I shall find Him and He is life everlasting."

By consenting to His will with joy and doing it with gladness I have His love in my heart, because my will is now the same as His love and I am on the way to becoming what He is, Who is Love. And by accepting all things from Him I receive His joy into my soul, not because things are what they are but because God is Who He is, and His love has willed my joy in them all.

How am I to know the will of God? Even where there is no other more explicit claim on my obedience, such as a legitimate command, the very nature of each situation usually bears written into itself some indication of God's will. For whatever is demanded by truth, by justice, by mercy, or by love must surely be taken to be willed by God. To consent to His will is, then, to consent to be true, or to speak truth, or at least to seek it. To obey Him is to respond to His will expressed in the need of another person, or at least to respect the rights of others. For the right of another man is the expression of God's love and God's will. In demanding that I respect the rights of another God is not merely asking me to conform to some abstract, arbitrary law: He is enabling me to share, as His son, in His own care for my brother. No man who ignores the rights and needs of others can hope to walk in the light of contemplation, because his way has turned aside from truth, from compassion and therefore from God.

The requirements of a work to be done can be understood as the will of God. If I am supposed to hoe a garden or make a table, then I will be obeying God if I am true to the task I am performing. To do the work carefully and well, with love and respect for the nature of my task and with due attention to its purpose, is to unite myself to God's will in my work. In this way I become His instrument. He works through me. When I act as His instrument my labor cannot become an obstacle to contemplation, even though it may temporarily so occupy my mind that I cannot engage in it while I am actually doing my job. Yet my work itself will purify and pacify my mind and dispose me for contemplation.

Unnatural, frantic, anxious work, work done under pressure of greed or fear or any other inordinate passion, cannot properly speaking be dedicated to God, because God never wills such work directly. He may permit that through no fault of our own we may have to work madly and distractedly, due to our sins, and to the sins of the society in which we live. In that case we must tolerate it and make the best of what we cannot avoid. But let us not be blind to the distinction between sound, healthy work and unnatural toil.

In any case, we should always seek to conform to the *logos* or truth of the duty before us, the work to be done, or our own God-given nature. Contemplative obedience and abandonment to the will of God can never mean a cultivated indifference to the natural values implanted by Him in human life and work. Insensitivity must not be confused with detachment. The contemplative must certainly be detached, but he can never allow himself to become insensible to true human values, whether in society, in other men or in himself. If he does so, then his contemplation stands condemned as vitiated in its very root.

IN SILENCE

Be still
Listen to the stones of the wall.
Be silent, they try
To speak your

Name.
Listen
To the living walls.
Who are you?
Who
Are you? Whose
Silence are you?

Who (be quiet)
Are you (as these stones
Are quiet). Do not
Think of what you are
Still less of
What you may one day be.
Rather
Be what you are (but who?) be

The unthinkable one
You do not know.

O be still, while
You are still alive,
And all things live around you
Speaking (I do not hear)
To your own being,
Speaking by the Unknown
That is in you and in themselves.

"I will try, like them
To be my own silence:
And this is difficult. The whole
World is secretly on fire. The stones
Burn, even the stones
They burn me. How can a man be still or
Listen to all things burning? How can he dare
To sit with them when
All their silence
Is on fire?"

PERFECT JOY

from the Chinese of Chuang Tzu

Is there to be found on earth a fullness of joy, or is there no such thing? Is there some way to make life fully worth living, or is this impossible? If there is such a way, how do you go about finding it? What should you try to do? What should you seek to avoid? What should be the goal in which your activity comes to rest? What should you accept? What should you refuse to accept? What should you love? What should you hate?

What the world values is money, reputation, long life, achievement. What it counts as joy is health and comfort of body, good food, fine clothes, beautiful things to look at, pleasant music to listen to.

What it condemns is lack of money, a low social rank, a reputation for being no good, and an early death.

What it considers misfortune is bodily discomfort and labor, no chance to get your fill of good food, not having good clothes to wear, having no way to amuse or delight the eye, no pleasant music to listen to. If people find that they are deprived of these things, they go into a panic or fall into despair. They are so concerned for their life that their anxiety makes life unbearable, even when they have the things they think they want. Their very concern for enjoyment makes them unhappy.

The rich make life intolerable, driving themselves in order to get more and more money which they cannot really use. In doing so they are alienated from themselves, and exhaust themselves in their own service as though they were slaves of others.

The ambitious run day and night in pursuit of honors, constantly in anguish about the success of their plans, dreading the miscalculation that may wreck everything. Thus they are alienated from themselves, exhausting their real life in service of the shadow created by their insatiable hope.

The birth of a man is the birth of his sorrow.

The longer he lives, the more stupid he

becomes, because his anxiety to avoid unavoidable death becomes more and more acute. What bitterness! He lives for what is always out of reach! His thirst for survival in the future makes him incapable of living in the present.

What about the self-sacrificing officials and scholars? They are honored by the world because they are good, upright, self-sacrificing men.

Yet their good character does not preserve them from unhappiness, nor even from ruin, disgrace, and death.

I wonder, in that case, if their "goodness" is really so good after all! Is it perhaps a source of unhappiness?

Suppose you admit they are happy. But is it a happy thing to have a character and a career that lead to one's own eventual destruction? On the other hand, can you call them "unhappy" if, in sacrificing themselves, they save the lives and fortunes of others?

Take the case of the minister who conscientiously and uprightly opposes an unjust decision of his king! Some say, "Tell the truth, and if the King will not listen, let him do what he likes. You have no further obligation."

On the other hand, Tzu Shu continued to resist the unjust policy of his sovereign. He was consequently destroyed. But if he had not stood up for what he believed to be right, his name would not be held in honor.

So there is the question, Shall the course he took be called "good" if, at the same time, it was fatal to him?

I cannot tell if what the world considers "happiness" is happiness or not. All I know is that when I consider the way they go about attaining it, I see them carried away headlong, grim and obsessed, in the general onrush of the human herd, unable to stop themselves or to change their direction. All the while they claim to be just on the point of attaining happiness.

For my part, I cannot accept their standards, whether of happiness or unhappiness. I ask myself if after all their concept of happiness has any meaning whatever.

My opinion is that you never find happiness until you stop looking for it. My greatest happiness consists precisely in doing nothing whatever that is calculated to obtain happiness: and this, in the minds of most people, is the worst possible course.

I will hold to the saying that: "Perfect joy is to be without joy. Perfect praise is to be without praise."

CUTTING UP AN OX

from the Chinese of Chuang Tzu

Prince Wen Hui's cook
Was cutting up an ox.
Out went a hand,
Down went a shoulder,
He planted a foot,
He pressed with a knee,
The ox fell apart
With a whisper,
The bright cleaver murmured
Like a gentle wind.
Rhythm! Timing!
Like a sacred dance,
Like "The Mulberry Grove,"
Like ancient harmonies!

"Good work!" the Prince exclaimed,
"Your method is faultless!"
"Method?" said the cook
Laying aside his cleaver,
"What I follow is Tao
Beyond all methods!

"When I first began
To cut up oxen
I would see before me
The whole ox
All in one mass.

"After three years
I no longer saw this mass.
I saw the distinctions.

"But now, I see nothing
With the eye. My whole being
Apprehends.
My senses are idle. The spirit
Free to work without plan
Follows its own instinct
Guided by natural line,
By the secret opening, the hidden space,
My cleaver finds its own way.
I cut through no joint, chop no bone.

"A good cook needs a new chopper
Once a year—he cuts.
A poor cook needs a new one
Every month—he hacks!

"I have used this same cleaver
Nineteen years.
It has cut up
A thousand oxen.
Its edge is as keen
As if newly sharpened.

"There are spaces in the joints;
The blade is thin and keen:
When this thinness
Finds that space
There is all the room you need!
It goes like a breeze!
Hence I have this cleaver nineteen years
As if newly sharpened!

“True, there are sometimes
Tough joints. I feel them coming,
I slow down, I watch closely,
Hold back, barely move the blade,
And whump! the part falls away
Landing like a clod of earth.

“Then I withdraw the blade,
I stand still
And let the joy of the work
Sink in.
I clean the blade
And put it away.”

Prince Wan Hui said,
“This is it! My cook has shown me
How I ought to live
My own life!”

Detachment from things does not mean setting up a contradiction between "things" and "God" as if God were another "thing" and as if His creatures were His rivals. We do not detach ourselves from things in order to attach ourselves to God, but rather we become detached *from ourselves* in order to see and use all things in and for God. This is an entirely new perspective which many sincerely moral and ascetic minds fail utterly to see. There is no evil in anything created by God, nor can anything of His become an obstacle to our union with Him. The obstacle is in our "self," that is to say in the tenacious need to maintain our separate, external, egotistic will. It is when we refer all things to this outward and false "self" that we alienate ourselves from reality and from God. It is then the false self that is our god, and we love everything for the sake of this self. We use all things, so to speak, for the worship of this idol which is our imaginary self. In so doing we pervert and corrupt things, or rather we turn our relationship to them into a corrupt and sinful relationship. We do not thereby make them evil, but we use them to increase our attachment to our illusory self.

Those who try to escape from this situation by treating the good things of God as if they were evils are only confirming themselves in a terrible illusion. They are like Adam blaming Eve and Eve blaming the serpent in Eden. "Woman has tempted me. Wine has tempted me. Food has tempted me. Woman is pernicious, wine is poison, food is death. I must hate and revile them. By hating them I will please God. . . ." These are the thoughts and attitudes of a baby, of a savage and of an idolater who seeks by magic incantations and spells to protect his egotistic self and placate the insatiable little god in his own heart. To take such an idol for God is the worst kind of self-deception. It turns a man into a fanatic, no longer capable of sustained contact with the truth, no longer capable of genuine love.

In trying to believe in their ego as something "holy" these fanatics look upon everything else as unholy.

It is not true that the saints and the great contemplatives never loved created things, and had no understanding or appreciation of the world, with its sights and sounds and the people living in it. They loved everything and everyone.

Do you think that their love of God was compatible with a hatred for things that reflected Him and spoke of Him on every side?

You will say that they were supposed to be absorbed in God and they had no eyes to see anything but Him. Do you think they walked around with faces like stones and did not listen to the voices of men speaking to them or understand the joys and sorrows of those who were around them?

It was because the saints were absorbed in God that they were truly capable of seeing and appreciating created things and it was because they loved Him alone that they alone loved everybody.

Some men seem to think that a saint cannot possibly take a natural interest in anything created. They imagine that any form of spontaneity or enjoyment is a sinful gratification of "fallen nature." That to be "supernatural" means obstructing all spontaneity with clichés and arbitrary references to God. The purpose of these clichés is, so to speak, to hold everything at arm's length, to frustrate spontaneous reactions, to exorcise feelings of guilt. Or perhaps to cultivate such feelings! One wonders sometimes if such morality is not after all a love of guilt! They suppose that the life of a saint can never be anything but a perpetual duel with guilt, and that a saint cannot even drink a glass of cold water without making an act of contrition for slaking his thirst, as if that were a mortal sin. As if for the saints every response to beauty, to goodness, to the pleasant, were an offense. As if the saint could never allow himself to be pleased with anything but his prayers and his interior acts of piety.

A saint is capable of loving created things and enjoying the use of them and dealing with them in a perfectly simple, natural manner, making no formal references to God, drawing no attention to his own piety, and acting without any artificial rigidity at all. His gentleness and his sweetness are not pressed through his pores by the crushing restraint of a spiritual strait-jacket. They come from his direct docility to the light of truth and to the will of God. Hence a saint is capable of talking about the world without any explicit reference to God, in such a way that his statement gives greater glory to God and arouses a greater love of God than the observations of someone less holy, who has to strain himself to make an arbitrary connection between creatures and God through the medium of hackneyed analogies and metaphors that are so feeble that they make you think there is something the matter with religion.

The saint knows that the world and everything made by God is good, while those who are not saints either think that created things are unholy, or else they don't bother about the question one way or another because they are only interested in themselves.

The eyes of the saint make all beauty holy and the hands of the saint consecrate everything they touch to the glory of God, and the saint is never offended by anything and judges no man's sin because he does not know sin. He knows the mercy of God. He knows that his own mission on earth is to bring that mercy to all men.

When we are one with God's love, we own all things in Him. They are ours to offer Him in Christ His Son. For all things belong to the sons of God and we are Christ's and Christ is God's. Resting in His glory above all pleasure and pain, joy or sorrow, and every other good or evil, we love in all things His will rather than the things themselves, and that is the way we make creation a sacrifice in praise of God.

This is the end for which all things were made by God.

The only true joy on earth is to escape from the prison of our own false self, and enter by love into union with the Life Who dwells and sings within the essence of every creature and in the core of our own souls. In His love we possess all things and enjoy fruition of them, finding Him in them all. And thus as we go about the world, everything we meet and everything we see and hear and touch, far from defiling, purifies us and plants in us something more of contemplation and of heaven.

Short of this perfection, created things do not bring us joy but pain. Until we love God perfectly, everything in the world will be able to hurt us. And the greatest misfortune is to be dead to the pain they inflict on us, and not to realize what it is.

For until we love God perfectly His world is full of contradiction. The things He has created attract us to Him and yet keep us away from Him. They draw us on and they stop us dead. We find Him in them to some extent and then we don't find Him in them at all.

Just when we think we have discovered some joy in them, the joy turns into sorrow; and just when they are beginning to please us the pleasure turns into pain.

In all created things we, who do not yet perfectly love God, can find something that reflects the fulfillment of heaven and something that reflects the anguish of hell. We find something of the joy of blessedness and something of the pain of loss, which is damnation.

The fulfillment we find in creatures belongs to the reality of the created being, a reality that is from God and belongs to God and reflects God. The anguish we find in them belongs to the disorder of our desire which looks for a greater reality in the object of our desire than is actually there: a greater fulfillment than any created thing is capable of giving. Instead of worshipping God through His creation we are always trying to worship ourselves by means of creatures.

But to worship our false selves is to worship nothing. And the worship of nothing is hell.

CAROL

Flocks feed by darkness with a noise of
whispers,
In the dry grass of pastures,
And lull the solemn night with their weak
bells.

The little towns upon the rocky hills
Look down as meek as children:
Because they have seen come this holy time.

God's glory, now, is kindled gentler than low
candlelight
Under the rafters of a barn:
Eternal Peace is sleeping in the hay,
And Wisdom's born in secret in a straw-
roofed stable.

And O! Make holy music in the stars, you
happy angels.
You shepherds, gather on the hill.

Look up, you timid flocks, where the three
kings
Are coming through the wintry trees;

While we unnumbered children of the
wicked centuries
Come after with our penances and prayers,
And lay them down in the sweet-smelling
hay
Beside the wise men's golden jars.

Everything good that comes to us and happens in prayer is a grace and a gift of God — even the desire to pray at all, and the attempt to pray, is itself a great grace. The mere fact of having an opportunity to pray is something for which we should be deeply grateful. St. Paul says that no one can call upon Jesus as Lord, truly, in his heart, without the grace of the Holy Spirit. Hence we can be certain that merely uttering the Holy Name with love is a pledge of great grace. If we learn to recognize all the little ordinary incidents of prayer as graces from God, and to thank Him humbly for them (not necessarily with a lot of words) we will appreciate the simplest and most ordinary "graces of prayer."...

Ardent aspirations of love sometimes arise in the soul more or less passively carrying it beyond all familiar forms of prayer to burning and inexpressible love for God which cannot express itself in words and for which there are no suitable concepts. This is what

Cassian calls the "prayer of fire." In the "flame" of this love all our other desires, yearnings, and aspirations are gathered together in one supreme striving to go out of ourselves in love for God and pay Him the homage of supreme adoration.

A brother asked one of the elders: What good thing shall I do, and have life thereby? The old man replied: God alone knows what is good. However, I have heard it said that someone inquired of Father Abbot Nisteros the great, the friend of Abbot Anthony, asking: What good work shall I do? and that he replied: Not all works are alike. For Scripture says that Abraham was hospitable and God was with him. Elias loved solitary prayer, and God was with him. And David was humble, and God was with him. Therefore, whatever you see your soul to desire according to God, do that thing, and you shall keep your heart safe.

*

An elder said: Cut off from yourself rash confidence, and control your tongue and your belly, and abstain from wine. And if anyone speak to you about any matter do not argue with him. But if he speaks rightly, say: Yes. If he speaks wrongly say to him: You know what you are saying. But do not argue with him about the things he has said. Thus your mind will be at peace.

*

A certain brother came to Abbot Silvanus at Mount Sinai, and seeing the hermits at work he exclaimed: Why do you work for the bread that perisheth? Mary has chosen the best part, namely to sit at the feet of the Lord without working. Then the Abbot said to his disciple Zachary: Give the brother a book and let him read, and put him in an empty cell. At the ninth hour the brother who was reading began to look out to see if the Abbot was not going to call him to dinner, and sometime after the ninth hour he went himself to the Abbot and said: Did the brethren not eat today, Father? Oh yes, certainly, said the Abbot, they just had dinner. Well, said the brother, why did you not call me? You are a spiritual man, said the elder, you don't need this food that perisheth. We have to work, but you have chosen the best part. You read all day, and can get along without food. Hearing this the brother said: Forgive me, Father. And the elder said: Martha is necessary to Mary, for it was because Martha worked that Mary was able to be praised.

*

A certain brother inquired of Abbot Pastor, saying: What shall I do? I lose my nerve when I am sitting alone at prayer in my cell? The elder said to him: Despise no one, condemn no one, rebuke no one, God will give you peace and your meditation will be undisturbed.

*

Abbot Ammonas said: One man carries an axe all his life and never cuts down a tree. Another, who knows how to cut, gives a few swings and the tree is down. This axe, he said, is discretion.

*

Abbot Pastor said: Get away from any man who always argues every time he talks.

*

A certain elder said: Apply yourself to silence, have no vain thoughts, and be intent in your meditation, whether you sit at prayer, or whether you rise up to work in the fear of God. If you do these things, you will not have to fear the attacks of the evil ones.

*

Abbot Lot came to Abbot Joseph and said: Father, according as I am able, I keep my little rule, and my little fast, my prayer, meditation and contemplative silence; and according as I am able I strive to cleanse my heart of thoughts: now what more should I do? The elder rose up in reply and stretched out his hands to heaven, and his fingers became like ten lamps of fire. He said: Why not be totally changed into fire?

*

A brother said to Abbot Pastor: If I give one of my brothers a little bread or something of the sort, the demons spoil everything and it seems to me that I have acted only to please men. The elder said to him: Even if your good work was done to please, we must still give to our brothers what they need. And he told him this story. Two farmers lived in a village. One of them sowed his field and reaped only a small and wretched crop. The other neglected to sow anything at all, and so he reaped nothing. Which of the two will survive, if there is a famine? The brother replied: The first one, even though his crop is small and wretched. The elder said to him: Let us also sow, even though our sowing is small and wretched, lest we die in the time of hunger.

*

One of the elders was asked what was humility, and he said: If you forgive a brother who has injured you before he himself asks pardon.

*

Abbot Anthony taught Abbot Ammonas, saying: You must advance yet further in the fear of God. And taking him out of the cell he showed him a stone, saying: Go and insult that stone, and beat it without ceasing. When this had been done, St. Anthony asked him if the stone had answered back. No, said Ammonas. Then Abbot Anthony said: You too must reach the point where you no longer take offense at anything.

*

Abbot Joseph asked Abbot Pastor: Tell me how I can become a monk. The elder replied: If you want to have rest here in this life and also in the next, in every conflict with another say: Who am I? And judge no one.

*

The same Abbot Agatho would say: Even if an angry man were to revive the dead, he would not be pleasing to God because of his anger.

*

Once there was a disciple of a Greek philosopher who was commanded by his Master for three years to give money to everyone who insulted him. When this period of trial was over, the Master said to him: Now you can go to Athens and learn wisdom. When the disciple was entering Athens he met a certain wise man who sat at the gate insulting everybody who came and went. He also insulted the disciple who immediately burst out laughing.

Why do you laugh when I insult you? said the wise man. Because, said the disciple, for three years I have been paying for this kind of thing and now you give it to me for nothing. Enter the city, said the wise man, it is all yours.

*

One of the elders said: A monk ought not to inquire how this one acts, or how that one lives. Questions like this take us away from prayer and draw us on to backbiting and chatter. There is nothing better than to keep silent.

SONG FOR NOBODY

A yellow flower
(Light and spirit)
Sings by itself
For nobody.

A golden spirit
(Light and emptiness)
Sings without a word
By itself.

Let no one touch this gentle sun
In whose dark eye
Someone is awake.

(No light, no gold, no name, no color
And no thought:
O, wide awake!)

A golden heaven
Sings by itself
A song to nobody.

FOR MY BROTHER:
REPORTED MISSING IN ACTION, 1943

Sweet brother, if I do not sleep
My eyes are flowers for your tomb;
And if I cannot eat my bread,

My fasts shall live like willows where you
        died.
If in the heat I find no water for my thirst,
My thirst shall turn to springs for you, poor
        traveller.

Where, in what desolate and smokey country,
Lies your poor body, lost and dead?
And in what landscape of disaster
Has your unhappy spirit lost its road?

Come, in my labor find a resting place
And in my sorrows lay your head,
Or rather take my life and blood
And buy yourself a better bed—
Or take my breath and take my death
And buy yourself a better rest.

When all the men of war are shot
And flags have fallen into dust,
Your cross and mine shall tell men still
Christ died on each, for both of us.

For in the wreckage of your April Christ lies
        slain,
And Christ weeps in the ruins of my spring:
The money of Whose tears shall fall
Into your weak and friendless hand,
And buy you back to your own land:
The silence of Whose tears shall fall
Like bells upon your alien tomb.
Hear them and come: they call you home.

THE EMPTY BOAT

from the Chinese of Chuang Tzu

If a man is crossing a river
And an empty boat collides with his own
skiff,
Even though he be a bad-tempered man
He will not become very angry.
But if he sees a man in the boat,
He will shout at him to steer clear.
If the shout is not heard, he will shout again,
And yet again, and begin cursing.
And all because there is somebody in the
boat.
Yet if the boat were empty,
He would not be shouting, and not angry.

If you can empty your own boat
Crossing the river of the world,
No one will oppose you,
No one will seek to harm you.

The straight tree is the first to be cut down,
The spring of clear water is the first to be
drained dry.

If you wish to improve your wisdom
And shame the ignorant,
To cultivate your character
And outshine others;
A light will shine around you
As if you had swallowed the sun and the
        moon:
You will not avoid calamity.

A wise man has said:

> "He who is content with himself
> Has done a worthless work.
> Achievement is the beginning of failure.
> Fame is the beginning of disgrace."

Who can free himself from achievement
And from fame, descend and be lost
Amid the masses of men?
He will flow like Tao, unseen,
He will go about like Life itself
With no name and no home.
Simple is he, without distinction.

To all appearances he is a fool.
His steps leave no trace. He has no power.
He achieves nothing, has no reputation.
Since he judges no one
No one judges him.
Such is the perfect man:
His boat is empty.

A tree gives glory to God by being a tree. For in being what God means it to be it is obeying Him. It "consents," so to speak, to His creative love. It is expressing an idea which is in God and which is not distinct from the essence of God, and therefore a tree imitates God by being a tree.

The more a tree is like itself, the more it is like Him. If it tried to be like something else which it was never intended to be, it would be less like God and therefore it would give Him less glory.

No two created beings are exactly alike. And their individuality is no imperfection. On the contrary, the perfection of each created thing is not merely in its conformity to an abstract type but in its own individual identity with itself. This particular tree will give glory to God by spreading out its roots in the earth and raising its branches into the air and the light in a way that no other tree before or after it ever did or will do.

Do you imagine that the individual created things in the world are imperfect attempts at reproducing an ideal type which the Creator never quite succeeded in actualizing on earth? If that is so they do not give Him glory but proclaim that He is not a perfect Creator.

Therefore each particular being, in its individuality, its concrete nature and entity, with all its own characteristics and its private qualities and its own inviolable identity, gives glory to God by being precisely what He wants it to be here and now, in the circumstances ordained for it by His Love and His infinite Art.

The forms and individual characters of living and growing things, of inanimate beings, of animals and flowers and all nature, constitute their holiness in the sight of God.

Their inscape is their sanctity. It is the imprint of His wisdom and His reality in them.

The special clumsy beauty of this particular colt on this April day in this field under these clouds is a holiness consecrated to God by His own creative wisdom and it declares the glory of God.

The pale flowers of the dogwood outside this window are saints. The little yellow flowers that nobody notices on the edge of that road are saints looking up into the face of God. This leaf has its own texture and its own pattern of veins and its own holy shape, and the bass and trout hiding in the deep pools of the river are canonized by their beauty and their strength.

The lakes hidden among the hills are saints, and the sea too is a saint who praises God without interruption in her majestic dance.

The great, gashed, half-naked mountain is another of God's saints. There is no other like him. He is alone in his own character; nothing else in the world ever did or ever will imitate God in quite the same way. That is his sanctity.

But what about you? What about me?

Unlike the animals and the trees, it is not enough for us to be what our nature intends. It is not enough for us to be individual men. For us, holiness is more than humanity. If we are never anything but men, never anything but people, we will not be saints and we will not be able to offer to God the worship of our imitation, which is sanctity.

It is true to say that for me sanctity consists in being myself and for you sanctity consists in being *your* self and that, in the last analysis, your sanctity will never be mine and mine will never be yours, except in the communism of charity and grace.

For me to be a saint means to be myself. Therefore the problem of sanctity and salvation is in fact the problem of finding out who I am and of discovering my true self.

Trees and animals have no problem. God makes them what they are without consulting them, and they are perfectly satisfied.

With us it is different. God leaves us free to be whatever we like. We can be ourselves or not, as we please. We are at liberty to be real, or to be unreal. We may be true or false, the choice is ours. We may wear now one mask and now another, and never, if we so desire, appear with our own true face. But we cannot make these choices with impunity. Causes have effects, and if we lie to ourselves and to others, then we cannot expect to find truth and reality whenever we happen to want them. If we have chosen the way of falsity we must not be surprised that truth eludes us when we finally come to need it!

Our vocation is not simply to *be*, but to work together with God in the creation of our own life, our own identity, our own destiny. We are free beings and sons of God. This means to say that we should not passively exist, but actively participate in His creative freedom, in our own lives, and in the lives of others, by choosing the truth. To put it better, we are even called to share with God the work of *creating* the truth of our identity. We can evade this responsibility by playing with masks, and this pleases us because it can appear at times to be a free and creative way of living. It is quite easy, it seems to please everyone. But in the long run the cost and the sorrow come very high. To work out our own identity in God, which the Bible calls "working out our salvation," is a labor that requires sacrifice and anguish, risk and many tears. It demands close attention to reality at every moment, and great fidelity to God as He reveals Himself, obscurely, in the mystery of each new situation. We do not know clearly beforehand what the result of this work will be. The secret of my full identity is hidden in Him. He alone can make me who I am, or rather who I will be when at last I fully begin to be. But unless I desire this identity and work to find it with Him and in Him, the work will never be done. The way of doing it is a secret I can learn from no one else but Him. There is no way of attaining to the secret without faith. But contemplation is the greater and more precious gift, for it enables me to see and understand the work that He wants done.

The seeds that are planted in my liberty at every moment, by God's will, are the seeds of my own identity, my own reality, my own happiness, my own sanctity.

To refuse them is to refuse everything; it is the refusal of my own existence and being: of my identity, my very self.

Not to accept and love and do God's will is to refuse the fullness of my existence.

If I never become what I am meant to be, but always remain what I am not, I shall spend eternity contradicting myself by being at once something and nothing, a life that wants to live and is dead, a death that wants to be dead and cannot quite achieve its own death because it still has to exist.

To say I was born in sin is to say I came into the world with a false self. I was born in a mask. I came into existence under a sign of contradiction, being someone that I was never intended to be and therefore a denial of what I am supposed to be. And thus I came into existence and nonexistence at the same time because from the very start I was something that I was not.

To say the same thing without paradox: as long as I am no longer anybody else than the thing that was born of my mother, I am so far short of being the person I ought to be that I might as well not exist at all. In fact, it were better for me that I had not been born.

Every one of us is shadowed by an illusory person: a false self.

This is the man that I want myself to be but who cannot exist, because God does not know anything about him. And to be unknown of God is altogether too much privacy.

My false and private self is the one who wants to exist outside the reach of God's will and God's love—outside of reality and outside of life. And such a self cannot help but be an illusion.

We are not very good at recognizing illusions, least of all the ones we cherish about ourselves—the ones we are born with and which feed the roots of sin. For most of the people in the world, there is no greater subjective reality than this false self of theirs, which cannot exist. A life devoted to the cult of this shadow is what is called a life of sin.

All sin starts from the assumption that my false self, the self that exists only in my own egocentric desires, is the fundamental reality of life to which everything else in the universe is ordered. Thus I use up my life in the desire for pleasures and the thirst for experiences, for power, honor, knowledge and love, to clothe this false self and construct its nothingness into something objectively real. And I wind experiences around myself and cover myself with pleasures and glory like bandages in order to make myself perceptible to myself and to the world, as if I were an invisible body that could only become visible when something visible covered its surface.

But there is no substance under the things with which I am clothed. I am hollow, and my structure of pleasures and ambitions has no foundation. I am objectified in them. But they are all destined by their very contingency to be destroyed. And when they are gone there will be nothing left of me but my own nakedness and emptiness and hollowness, to tell me that I am my own mistake.

The secret of my identity is hidden in the love and mercy of God.

But whatever is in God is really identical with Him, for His infinite simplicity admits no division and no distinction. Therefore I cannot hope to find myself anywhere except in Him.

Ultimately the only way that I can be myself is to become identified with Him in Whom is hidden the reason and fulfillment of my existence.

Therefore there is only one problem on

which all my existence, my peace and my happiness depend: to discover myself in discovering God. If I find Him I will find myself and if I find my true self I will find Him.

But although this looks simple, it is in reality immensely difficult. In fact, if I am left to myself it will be utterly impossible. For although I can know something of God's existence and nature by my own reason, there is no human and rational way in which I can arrive at that contact, that possession of Him, which will be the discovery of Who He really is and of Who I am in Him.

That is something that no man can ever do alone.

Nor can all the men and all the created things in the universe help him in this work.

The only One Who can teach me to find God is God, Himself, Alone.

THE WOODCARVER

from the Chinese of Chuang Tzu

Khing, the master carver, made a bell stand
Of precious wood. When it was finished,
All who saw it were astounded. They said it
must be
The work of spirits.
The Prince of Lu said to the master carver:
"What is your secret?"

Khing replied: "I am only a workman:
I have no secret. There is only this:
When I began to think about the work you
commanded
I guarded my spirit, did not expend it
On trifles, that were not to the point.
I fasted in order to set
My heart at rest.
After three days fasting,
I had forgotten gain and success.
After five days
I had forgotten praise or criticism.
After seven days

I had forgotten my body
With all its limbs.

"By this time all thought of your Highness
And of the court had faded away.
All that might distract me from the work
Had vanished.
I was collected in the single thought
Of the bell stand.

"Then I went to the forest
To see the trees in their own natural state.
When the right tree appeared before my
eyes,
The bell stand also appeared in it, clearly,
beyond doubt.
All I had to do was to put forth my hand
And begin.

"If I had not met this particular tree
There would have been
No bell stand at all.

“What happened?
My own collected thought
Encountered the hidden potential in the
        wood;
From this live encounter came the work
Which you ascribe to the spirits.”

"WHEN IN THE SOUL OF THE SERENE DISCIPLE . . ."

When in the soul of the serene disciple
With no more Fathers to imitate
Poverty is a success,
It is a small thing to say the roof is gone:
He has not even a house.

Stars, as well as friends,
Are angry with the noble ruin.
Saints depart in several directions.

Be still:
There is no longer any need of comment.
It was a lucky wind
That blew away his halo with his cares,
A lucky sea that drowned his reputation.

Here you will find
Neither a proverb nor a memorandum.
There are no ways,
No methods to admire
Where poverty is no achievement.

His God lives in his emptiness like an
        affliction.

What choice remains?
Well, to be ordinary is not a choice:
It is the usual freedom
Of men without visions.

Solitude is not found so much by looking outside the boundaries of your dwelling, as by staying within. Solitude is not something you must hope for in the future. Rather, it is a deepening of the present, and unless you look for it in the present you will never find it.

TRAPPISTS, WORKING

Now all our saws sing holy sonnets in this
 world of timber
Where oaks go off like guns, and fall like
 cataracts,
Pouring their roar into the wood's green well.

Walk to us, Jesus, through the wall of trees,
And find us still adorers in these airy
 churches,
Singing our other Office with our saws and
 axes.
Still teach Your children in the busy forest,
And let some little sunlight reach us, in our
 mental shades, and leafy studies.

When time has turned the country white
 with grain
And filled our regions with the thrashing sun,
Walk to us, Jesus, through the walls of wheat
When our two tractors come to cut them
 down:

Sow some light winds upon the acres of our
    spirit,
And cool the regions where our prayers are
    reapers,
And slake us, Heaven, with Your living rivers.

THE TIME OF THE END IS THE TIME OF NO ROOM

Note: *In its Biblical sense, the expression "the End" does not necessarily mean only "the violent, sudden and bad end." Biblical eschatology must not be confused with the vague and anxious eschatology of human foreboding. We live in an age of two superimposed eschatologies: that of secular anxieties and hopes, and that of revealed fulfillment. Sometimes the first is merely mistaken for the second, sometimes it results from complete denial and despair of the second. In point of fact the pathological* fear of the violent end *which, when sufficiently aroused, actually becomes a thinly disguised* hope for the violent end, *provides something of the climate of confusion and despair in which the more profound hopes of Biblical eschatology are realized—for everyone is forced to confront* the possibility, *and to accept or reject them. This definitive confrontation is precisely what Biblical eschatology announces to us. In speaking of "the time of the End," we keep in mind both these levels of meaning. But it should be clear that for the author, there is no question of prognostication or Apocalypse—only a sober statement about the climate of our time, a time of finality and of fulfillment.*

When the perfect and ultimate message, the joy which is *The Great Joy*, explodes silently upon the world, there is no longer any room for sadness. Therefore no circumstance in the Christmas Gospel, however trivial it may seem, is to be left out of The Great Joy. In the special and heavenly light which shines around the coming of the Word into the world, all ordinary things are transfigured. In the mystery of Peace which is proclaimed to a world that cannot believe in peace, a world of suspicion, hatred and distrust, even the rejection of the Prince of Peace takes on something of the color and atmosphere of peace.

So there was no room at the inn? True! But that is simply mentioned in passing, in a matter of fact sort of way, as the Evangelist points to what he really means us to see—the picture of pure peace, pure joy: "She wrapped her first born Son in swaddling clothes and laid him in the manger" (Luke 2:7). By now we know it well, and yet we all might still be questioning it—except that a reason was given for an act that might otherwise have seemed strange: "there was no room for them at the inn." Well, then, they obviously found some other place!

But when we read the Gospels and come to know them thoroughly, we realize there are other reasons why it was necessary that there be no room at the inn, and why there had to be some other place. In fact, the inn was the last place in the world for the birth of the Lord.

The Evangelists, preparing us for the announcement of the birth of the Lord, remind us that the fullness of time has come. Now is the time of final decision, the time of mercy, the "acceptable time," the time of settlement, the time of the end. It is the time of repentance, the time for the fulfillment of all promises, for the Promised One has come. But with the coming of the end, a great bustle and business begins to shake the nations of the world. The time of the end is the time of massed armies, "wars and rumors of wars," of huge crowds moving this way and that, of "men withering away for fear," of flaming cities and sinking fleets, of smoking lands laid waste, of technicians planning grandiose acts of destruction. The time of the end is the time of the Crowd: and the eschatological message is spoken in a world where, precisely because of the vast indefinite roar of armies on the move and the restlessness of turbulent mobs, the message can be heard only with difficulty. Yet it is heard by those who are aware that the display of power, *hubris* and destruction is part of the *kerygma*. That which is to be judged announces itself, introduces itself by its sinister and arrogant claim to absolute power. Thus it is identified, and those who decide in favor of this claim are numbered, marked with the sign of power, aligned with power, and destroyed with it.

Why then was the inn crowded? Because of the census, the eschatological massing of the "*whole world*" in centers of registration, to be numbered, to be identified with the structure of imperial power. The purpose of the census: to discover those who were to be taxed. To find out those who were eligible for service in the armies of the empire.

The Bible had not been friendly to a census in the days when God was the ruler of Israel (II Samuel 24). The numbering of the people of God by an alien emperor and their full consent to it was itself an eschatological sign, preparing those who could understand it to meet judgment with repentance. After all, in the Apocalyptic literature of the Bible, this "summoning together" or convocation of the powers of the earth to do battle is the great sign of "the end." For then "the demon spirits that work wonders go out to the Kings all over the world to muster them for battle on the great Day of God Almighty" (Revelations 16:14). And "the Beasts and the Kings of the earth and their armies gathered to make war upon him who was mounted on the horse and on his army" (Revelations 19:19). Then all the birds of prey gather from all sides in response to the angel's cry: "Gather for God's great banquet, and eat the bodies of Kings, commanders and mighty men, of horses and their riders...." (Revelations 19:18).

It was therefore impossible that the Word should lose Himself by being born into shapeless and passive mass. He had indeed emptied

Himself, taken the form of God's servant, man. But he did not empty Himself to the point of becoming mass man, faceless man. It was therefore right that there should be no room for him in a crowd that had been called together as an eschatological sign. His being born outside that crowd is even more of a sign. That there is no room for Him is a sign of the end.

Nor are the tidings of great joy announced in the crowded inn. In the massed crowd there are always new tidings of joy and disaster. Where each new announcement is the greatest of announcements, where every day's disaster is beyond compare, every day's danger demands the ultimate sacrifice, all news and all judgment is reduced to zero. News becomes merely a new noise in the mind, briefly replacing the noise that went before it and yielding to the noise that comes after it, so that eventually everything blends into the same monotonous and meaningless rumor. News? There is so much news that there is no room left for the true tidings, the "Good News," *The Great Joy*.

Hence The Great Joy is announced, after all, in silence, loneliness and darkness, to shepherds "living in the fields" or "living in the countryside" and apparently unmoved by the rumors or massed crowds. These are the remnant of the desert-dwellers, the nomads, the true Israel.

Even though "the whole world" is ordered to be inscribed, they do not seem to be affected. Doubtless they have registered, as Joseph and Mary will register, but they remain outside the agitation, and untouched by the vast movement, the massing of hundreds and thousands of people everywhere in the towns and cities.

They are therefore quite otherwise signed. They are designated, surrounded by a great light, they receive the message of The Great Joy, and they believe it with joy. They see the Shekinah over them, recognize themselves for what they are. They are the remnant, the people of no account, who are therefore chosen—the *anawim*. And they obey the light. Nor was anything else asked of them.

They go and they see not a prophet, not a spirit, but the Flesh in which the glory of the Lord will be revealed and by which all men will be delivered from the power that is in the world, the power that seeks to destroy the world because the world is God's creation, the power that mimics creation, and in doing so, pillages and exhausts the resources of a bounteous God-given earth.

We live in the time of no room, which is the time of the end. The time when everyone is obsessed with lack of time, lack of space, with saving time, conquering space, projecting into time and space the anguish produced within them by the technological furies of size, volume, quantity, speed, number, price, power and acceleration.

*

The time of the end? All right: when?

That is not the question.

To say it is the time of the end is to answer all the questions, for if it is the time of the end, and of great tribulation, then it is certainly and above all the time of The Great Joy. It is the time to "lift up your heads for your redemption is at hand." It is the time when the promise will be manifestly fulfilled, and no longer kept secret from anyone. It is the time for the joy that is given not as the world gives, and that no man can take away.

For the true eschatological banquet is not that of the birds on the bodies of the slain. It is the feast of the living, the wedding banquet of the Lamb. The true eschatological convocation is not the crowding of armies on the field of battle, but the summons of The Great Joy, the cry of deliverance: "Come out of her my people that you may not share in her sins and suffer from her plagues!" (Revelations 18:4). The cry of the time of the end was uttered also in the beginning by Lot in Sodom, to his sons-in-law: "Come, get out of this city, for the Lord will destroy it. But he seemed to them to be jesting" (Genesis 19:14).

To leave the city of death and imprisonment is surely not bad news except to those who have so identified themselves with their captivity that they can conceive no other reality and no other condition. In such a case, there is nothing but tribulation: for while to stay in captivity is tragic, to break away from it is unthinkable—and so more tragic still.

What is needed then is the grace and

courage to see that "The Great Tribulation" and "The Great Joy" are really inseparable, and that the "Tribulation" becomes "Joy" when it is seen as the Victory of Life over Death.

True, there is a sense in which there is no room for Joy in this tribulation. To say there is "no room" for The Great Joy in the tribulation of "the end" is to say that the Evangelical joy must not be confused with the joys proposed by the world in the time of the end—and, we must admit it, these are no longer convincing as joys. They become now stoic duties and sacrifices to be offered without question for ends that cannot be descried just now, since there is too much smoke and the visibility is rather poor. In the last analysis, the "joy" proposed by the time of the end is simply the satisfaction and the relief of getting it all over with....

That is the demonic temptation of "the end." For eschatology is not *finis* and punishment, the winding up of accounts and the closing of books: it is the final beginning, the definitive birth into a new creation. It is not the last gasp of exhausted possibilities but the first taste of all that is beyond conceiving as actual.

But can we believe it? ("He seemed to them to be jesting!")

A PSALM

When psalms surprise me with their music
And antiphons turn to rum
The Spirit sings: the bottom drops out of my
        soul

And from the center of my cellar, Love,
        louder than thunder
Opens a heaven of naked air.

New eyes awaken.
I send Love's name into the world with wings
And songs grow up around me like a jungle.
Choirs of all creatures sing the tunes
Your Spirit played in Eden.

Zebras and antelopes and birds of paradise
Shine on the face of the abyss
And I am drunk with the great wilderness
Of the sixth day in Genesis.

But sound is never half so fair
As when that music turns to air
And the universe dies of excellence.

Sun, moon and stars
Fall from their heavenly towers.
Joys walk no longer down the blue world's
shore.

Though fires loiter, lights still fly on the air of
the gulf,
All fear another wind, another thunder:
Then one more voice
Snuffs all their flares in one gust.

And I go forth with no more wine and no
more stars
And no more buds and no more Eden
And no more animals and no more sea:
While God sings by Himself in acres of night
And walls fall down, that guarded Paradise.

We have the choice of two identities: the external mask which seems to be real and which lives by a shadowy autonomy for the brief moment of earthly existence, and the hidden, inner person who seems to us to be nothing, but who can give himself eternally to the truth in whom he subsists. It is this inner self that is taken up into the mystery of Christ, by His love, by the Holy Spirit, so that in secret we live "in Christ."

Yet we must not deal in too negative a fashion even with the "external self." This self is not by nature evil, and the fact that it is unsubstantial is not to be imputed to it as some kind of crime. It is afflicted with metaphysical poverty: but all that is poor deserves mercy. So too our outward self: as long as it does not isolate itself in a lie, it is blessed by the mercy and the love of Christ. Appearances are to be accepted for what they are. The accidents of a poor and transient existence have, nevertheless, an ineffable value. They can be transparent media in which we apprehend the presence of God in the world. It is possible to speak of the exterior self as a mask: to do so is not necessarily to reprove it. The mask that each man wears may well be a disguise not only for that man's inner self but for God, wandering as a pilgrim and exile in His own creation.

And indeed, if Christ became Man, it is because He wanted to be any man and every man. If we believe in the Incarnation of the Son of God, there should be no one on earth in whom we are not prepared to see, in mystery, the presence of Christ.

What is serious to men is often very trivial in the sight of God. What in God might appear to us as "play" is perhaps what He Himself takes most seriously. At any rate the Lord plays and diverts Himself in the garden of His creation, and if we could let go of our own obsession with what we think is the meaning of it all, we might be able to hear His call and follow Him in His mysterious, cosmic dance. We do not have to go very far to catch echoes of that game, and of that dancing. When we are alone on a starlit night; when by chance we see the migrating birds in autumn descending on a grove of junipers to rest and eat; when we see children in a moment when they are really children; when we know love in our own hearts; or when, like the Japanese poet Bashō we hear an old frog land in a quiet pond with a solitary splash—at such times the awakening, the turning inside out of all values, the "newness," the emptiness and the purity of vision that make themselves evident, provide a glimpse of the cosmic dance.

For the world and time are the dance of the Lord in emptiness. The silence of the spheres is the music of a wedding feast. The more we persist in misunderstanding the phenomena of life, the more we analyze them out into strange finalities and complex purposes of our own, the more we involve ourselves in sadness, absurdity and despair. But it does not matter much, because no despair of ours can alter the reality of things, or stain the joy of the cosmic dance which is always there. Indeed, we are in the midst of it, and it is in the midst of us, for it beats in our very blood, whether we want it to or not.

Yet the fact remains that we are invited to forget ourselves on purpose, cast our awful solemnity to the winds and join in the general dance.

ADVENT

Charm with your stainlessness these winter
        nights,
Skies, and be perfect!
Fly vivider in the fiery dark, you quiet
        meteors,
And disappear.
You moon, be slow to go down,
This is your full!

The four white roads make off in silence
Towards the four parts of the starry universe.
Time falls like manna at the corners of the
        wintry earth.
We have become more humble than the
        rocks,
More wakeful than the patient hills.

Charm with your stainlessness these nights
        in Advent, holy spheres,
While minds, as meek as beasts,
Stay close at home in the sweet hay;

And intellects are quieter than the flocks that
    feed by starlight.

Oh pour your darkness and your brightness
    over all our solemn valleys,
You skies: and travel like the gentle Virgin,
Toward the planets' stately setting,

Oh white full moon as quiet as Bethlehem!

God is present, and His thought is alive and awake in the fullness and depth and breadth of all the silences of the world. The Lord is watching in the almond trees, over the fulfillment of His words (Jeremias 1:11).

Whether the planes pass by tonight or tomorrow, whether there be cars on the winding road or no cars, whether men speak in the field, whether there be a radio in the house or not, the tree brings forth her blossoms in silence.

Whether the house be empty or full of children, whether the men go off to town or work with tractors in the fields, whether the liner enters the harbor full of tourists or full of soldiers, the almond tree brings forth her fruit in silence.

THE FLOWER OF THE FRUIT

translated from the Spanish of Alfonso Cortés

In the silence of flowers is found a sacred love
That changes the future.
Being is, for its own road, the end
If some grace grants it
Fragrance and quiet.

Sweet blood explodes upon the tongue
When you break
The body of the fruit:
This is the word, vivid and absolute
With which each tree tries out its virtue.

Man is mystic tree and barely grasps
Space and Time if he can turn himself
Into soul's flower and veins' fruit;

For, from his double essence, unconfused
The bees of death draw honey
And the roses of life their fragrance.

O SWEET IRRATIONAL WORSHIP

Wind and a bobwhite
And the afternoon sun.

By ceasing to question the sun
I have become light,

Bird and wind.

My leaves sing.

I am earth, earth

All these lighted things
Grow from my heart.

A tall, spare pine
Stands like the initial of my first
Name when I had one.

When I had a spirit,
When I was on fire
When this valley was

Made out of fresh air
You spoke my name
In naming Your silence:
O sweet, irrational worship!

I am earth, earth

My heart's love
Bursts with hay and flowers.
I am a lake of blue air
In which my own appointed place
Field and valley
Stand reflected.

I am earth, earth

Out of my grass heart
Rises the bobwhite.

Out of my nameless weeds
His foolish worship.

SOURCES

"Seeds of Contemplation," from *New Seeds of Contemplation*, copyright © 1961 by the Abbey of Gethsemani, Inc.

"In Silence," from *The Collected Poems of Thomas Merton*, copyright © 1957 by the Abbey of Gethsemani, Inc.

"Perfect Joy," from *The Way of Chuang Tzu*, copyright © 1965 by the Abbey of Gethsemani.

"Cutting Up an Ox," from *The Way of Chuang Tzu*, copyright © 1965 by the Abbey of Gethsemani.

"Everything that Is, Is Holy," from *New Seeds of Contemplation*, copyright © 1961 by the Abbey of Gethsemani, Inc.

"Carol," from *The Collected Poems of Thomas Merton*, copyright © 1946 by New Directions Publishing Corp.

"Notes on Meditation," from *On Christian Contemplation*, copyright © 2012 by the Trustees of the Merton Legacy Trust.

Selections from *The Wisdom of the Desert*, copyright © 1960 by the Abbey of Gethsemani, Inc.

"Song for Nobody," from *The Collected Poems of Thomas Merton*, copyright © 1963 by the Abbey of Gesthemani, Inc.

"For My Brother: Reported Missing in Action, 1943," from *The Collected Poems of Thomas Merton*, copyright © 1944 by Our Lady of Gethsemani Monastery.

"The Empty Boat," from *The Way of Chuang Tzu*, copyright © 1965 by the Abbey of Gethsemani.

"Things in Their Identity," from *New Seeds of Contemplation*, copyright © 1961 by the Abbey of Gethsemani, Inc.

"The Woodcarver," from *The Way of Chuang Tzu*, copyright © 1965 by the Abbey of Gethsemani.

"When in the Soul of the Serene Disciple ...," from *The Collected Poems of Thomas Merton*, copyright © 1957 by the Abbey of Gethsemani, Inc.

"Solitude is not found so ...": excerpts from *The Sign of Jonas* by Thomas Merton. Copyright © 1953 by the Abbey of Our Lady of Gethsemani and renewed by the Trustees of the Merton Legacy Trust. Reprinted by permission of Houghton Mifflin Harcourt Publishing Company. All rights reserved.

"Trappists, Working," from *The Collected Poems of Thomas Merton*, copyright © 1946 by New Directions Publishing Corp.

"The Time of the End is the Time of No Room," from *Raids on the Unspeakable*, copyright © 1965 by the Abbey of Gethsemani, Inc.

"A Psalm," from *The Collected Poems of Thomas Merton*, copyright © 1949 by Our Lady of Gethsemani Monastery.

"The General Dance," from *New Seeds of Contemplation*, copyright © 1961 by the Abbey of Gethsemani, Inc.

"Advent," from *The Collected Poems of Thomas Merton*, copyright © 1946 by New Directions Publishing Corp.

"Silence": excerpt from *No Man is an Island* by Thomas Merton. Copyright © 1955 by the Abbey of Our Lady of Gethsemani and renewed 1983 by the Trustees of the Merton Legacy Trust. Reprinted by permission of Houghton Mifflin Harcourt Publishing Company. All rights reserved.

"The Flower of the Fruit," from *The Collected Poems of Thomas Merton*, copyright © 1977 by the Trustees of the Merton Legacy Trust.

"O Sweet Irrational Worship," from *The Collected Poems of Thomas Merton*, copyright © 1963 by the Abbey of Gethsemani, Inc.